INVESTIGATING
Conspiracy Theories

A Fake Moon Landing, Alien Life Secrets, AND MORE CONSPIRACY THEORIES ABOUT SPACE

by Nick Hunter

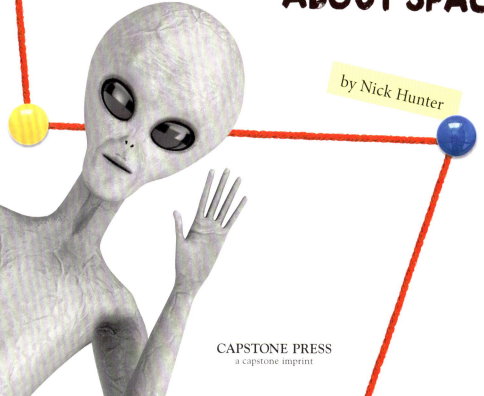

CAPSTONE PRESS
a capstone imprint

Published by Capstone Press, an imprint of Capstone
1710 Roe Crest Drive, North Mankato, Minnesota 56003
capstonepub.com

Copyright © 2025 by Capstone. All rights reserved. No part of this publication may be reproduced in whole or in part, or stored in a retrieval system, or transmitted in any form or by any means, electronic, mechanical, photocopying, recording, or otherwise, without written permission of the publisher.

Library of Congress Cataloging-in-Publication Data is available on the Library of Congress website.
ISBN: 9781669077404 (hardcover)
ISBN: 9781669077350 (paperback)
ISBN: 9781669077367 (ebook PDF)

Summary: Was the Apollo 11 moon landing in July 1969 faked? Is proof that aliens are real being kept hidden? People believe in many conspiracy theories about space. Get the inside story on each theory to discover why people believe in it and what scientists and experts have to say. Can these conspiracy theories be easily debunked, or will questions remain?

Editorial Credits
Editor: Carrie Sheely; Designer: Jaime Willems; Media Researcher: Svetlana Zhurkin; Production Specialist: Whitney Schaefer

Image Credits
Capstone: Jaime Willems (doodles), cover, back cover, and throughout; Getty Images: ESA, 21, 22, 23, imagenavi, 7, MPI, 19, New York Daily News, 8, Science Photo Library/Mark Garlick, 24; NASA: cover (middle left), 4, 5, 11, 12, 28, GSFC, 13, JPL-Caltech, 18, JPL-Caltech/MSSS, 17, JPL/Malin Space Science Systems, 16; Shutterstock: Dima Zel, 25, doomu (alien), cover, back cover, 1, Luca9257, 27, Mega Pixel (yellow paper), cover, back cover, and throughout, Nikolay Suchkov (color pins), cover, back cover, and throughout, Paitoon Pornsuksomboon, 9, pics five (string and crumpled paper), cover, back cover, and throughout, Skylines (instant photo), cover and throughout, Stockbym, 14, Vadim Sadovski, 29; Superstock: Image Asset Management/World History Archive, 15

Any additional websites and resources referenced in this book are not maintained, authorized, or sponsored by Capstone. All product and company names are trademarks™ or registered® trademarks of their respective holders.

Printed and bound in China. PO 5827

TABLE OF CONTENTS

Chapter 1
What Are Conspiracy Theories? 4

Chapter 2
Faked Moon Landing 8

Chapter 3
Alien Life Secrets 14

Chapter 4
Comet Cover-up 20

Chapter 5
Nemesis, Asteroids, and Remaining Questions 24

   Glossary 30
   Read More 31
   Internet Sites 31
   Index 32
   About the Author 32

Words in **BOLD** are in the glossary.

Chapter 1
WHAT ARE CONSPIRACY THEORIES?

Imagine you are an astronaut on the International Space Station (ISS). You're more than 240 miles (386 kilometers) above Earth's surface. As you look out a window, you see Earth. You're with a small team of astronauts doing experiments to learn more about living in space.

Astronauts looking out of the International Space Station can see 16 sunrises and sunsets a day.

The International Space Station in orbit around Earth

Since the ISS launched in 1998, photos and videos have shown what the astronauts do aboard it. But some people say these photos and videos are faked. Believers in this idea say the photos and videos are taken here on Earth. They say videos show the astronauts wearing harnesses and wires. The conspiracy theory supporters say this equipment is used to fake that they are floating in space with weaker **gravity**. Video **glitches** are said to be **evidence** that videos have been changed.

The conspiracy theorists also point out bubbles on some pictures and videos. They say the bubbles show that the astronauts are being filmed underwater.

5

EXPLANATIONS FROM EXPERTS

The National Aeronautics and Space Administration (NASA) has explained some of the points the conspiracy theory supporters have made. The wires are linked to headsets and microphones the astronauts need. The videos with bubbles were filmed during astronaut training in water tanks on Earth. This underwater training helps astronauts know what being weightless is like. Glitches are normal when videos are being sent from space. The conspiracy theory has been proven false.

SECRET PLOTS

A conspiracy theory says that there is a secret plot keeping people from knowing the truth. Conspiracy theories often say that the government or other people in power are trying to mislead us. Those who believe in these theories reject accepted explanations and **evidence**.

There are many conspiracy theories about space. They involve planets, the moon, and more. Let's launch into some of the most interesting and outrageous space conspiracy theories!

Questions to Ask About Conspiracy Theories

When you find out about a conspiracy theory, do research. Learn as much as you can. It's important not to assume a conspiracy theory is true. Many conspiracy theories can be proven false. For others, parts of them may be true.

- What evidence supports this theory? Ask if there are reliable sources or scientific studies that provide evidence for the claims.
- Who is saying this? What are the sources of information? Consider whether the sources are trustworthy.
- Are there other explanations? Consider different viewpoints. Think critically and weigh different possibilities.
- Has this theory been widely accepted or rejected by experts? Understand the value of expert opinions and scientific evidence. Theories that are widely accepted by experts are generally more reliable than those supported by a few individuals or groups.

Chapter 2

FAKED MOON LANDING

On July 20, 1969, millions of people around the world watched in amazement as American astronaut Neil Armstrong took the first steps on the moon. Thousands of people had worked for eight years to put a human on the moon. It was one of the greatest achievements in history. Yet some people believe in a conspiracy theory that says the Apollo 11 moon landing was faked.

People at John F. Kennedy Airport in New York watch the Apollo 11 moon landing.

Former U.S. Navy officer Bill Kaysing had worked for a company that built rockets for the space program. In 1976, his book was published. It said there was a government plot to fake the first moon landing. Many people believed Kaysing's claims.

According to the conspiracy theory, NASA launched a spacecraft into **orbit** around Earth. But it wasn't able to send the spacecraft to the moon. Believers in the conspiracy theory say images of Armstrong and Buzz Aldrin on the moon were taken on a movie set.

WHAT'S THE EVIDENCE?

Believers in this conspiracy theory point to clues that the Apollo 11 moon landing was staged. First, there are no stars in the dark sky of the photos. Some shadows in photos of the moon landing are not **parallel**. People say it appears they were made by light sources other than the sun. Conspiracy theory supporters question why the U.S. flag the astronauts planted on the moon seems to be waving in the wind. The moon has no **atmosphere**, so there is no wind.

Scientists have responded to the points conspiracy theory supporters have made. They say the surface of the moon is very bright. For this reason, stars do not show up in the photos. The non-parallel appearance of the shadows happens on Earth too. This does not mean there is a light source other than the sun. The flag seems to wave because it is attached to a rod at the top.

Aldrin stands next to the flag the astronauts planted on the moon.

There is other evidence that astronauts visited the moon. The Apollo 11 astronauts brought back more than 45 pounds (20 kilograms) of rocks and dust from the moon. Labs around the world confirmed the rocks were from the moon. Astronauts also left behind footprints, the flag, and other items. Highly detailed photos from NASA's Lunar Reconnaissance Orbiter (LRO) have shown moon landing sites and equipment left there.

Moon rocks collected by Armstrong and Aldrin

Fact

Around 400,000 people worked on the Apollo 11 mission. If the moon landing was faked, they would have had to keep it secret.

Some instruments on the LRO give scientists information about the moon's surface.

THE CONSPIRACY THEORY LIVES ON

Many people were convinced by the fake moon landing theory when it first appeared in the 1970s. Trust in the U.S. government was low. Many people didn't believe that technology was advanced enough to land people on the moon. Today, the conspiracy theory is still widely discussed on the internet. Surveys show that around one in 20 Americans believe the conspiracy theory, despite evidence that proves the landing did occur.

Chapter 3

ALIEN LIFE SECRETS

Do you believe there is life on other planets? Officially, scientists have found no clear signs of life anywhere in the universe. However, many people believe governments are keeping evidence of alien life secret. Are we being told the whole truth?

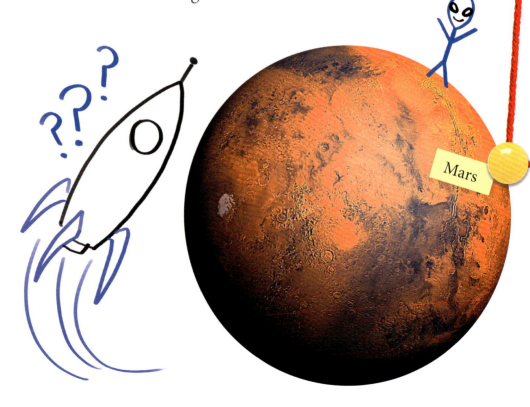

Mars

In 1976, NASA's Viking 1 mission sent detailed pictures of Mars. When people studied them, they could see an area of the surface that looked like a human face. People wrote about the face in books and magazines. It was suggested that the face could be a signal from an alien civilization. Author Richard C. Hoagland claimed that the face and other unusual rock formations were buildings from a Martian city.

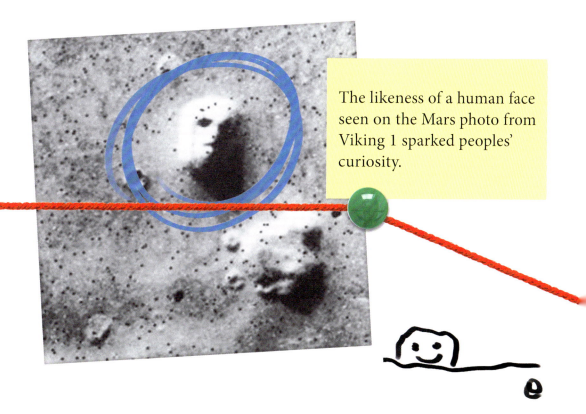

The likeness of a human face seen on the Mars photo from Viking 1 sparked peoples' curiosity.

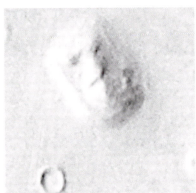

The Mars Orbiter Camera took a photo of the Mars face in 1998. When enhanced, the image helped people see the face was a natural formation.

MORE QUESTIONS

NASA said the face was just a natural rock formation. Shadows from the sun made it look like a face. Later photographs of the area have proven NASA's explanation. But questions about life on Mars did not stop there.

By 2022, NASA's Curiosity **rover** was sending back very clear images from Mars. One picture seemed to show a rectangular doorway carved into a rock. Conspiracy theorists claimed that the doorway and nearby rocks looked unnatural. NASA was quick to say this was a natural rock feature.

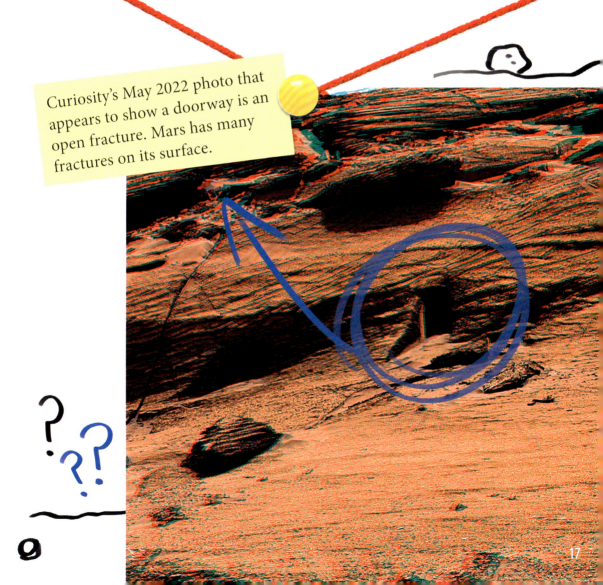

Curiosity's May 2022 photo that appears to show a doorway is an open fracture. Mars has many fractures on its surface.

People who have studied photos from Mars have reported seeing other features and signs of life. In 2019, a former college professor was studying photos from Mars. He said they showed insect-like creatures.

People who believe in the conspiracy theory say evidence of alien life is being covered up. NASA scientists say that they don't know of any alien life on other planets yet. But they continue to search for it.

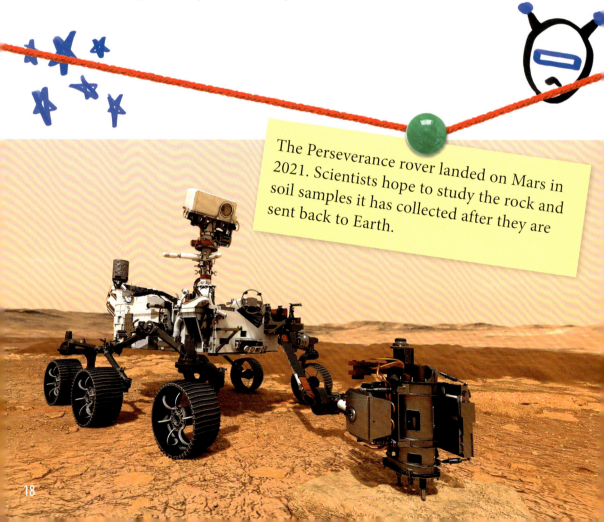

The Perseverance rover landed on Mars in 2021. Scientists hope to study the rock and soil samples it has collected after they are sent back to Earth.

The Viking 1 lander took the first color picture of Mars' surface in 1976.

Tiny Signs of Life

NASA scientist Gilbert Levin worked on the Viking 1 mission in 1976. In an experiment on that mission, soil samples on Mars were tested for signs of life. The results showed signs that small living things called **microbes** were in the samples. Later experiments on the samples failed to show these signs. Most scientists think that no life was present. However, if life is found on Mars in the future, scientists think it's likely to be microscopic.

Chapter 4
COMET COVER-UP

In 2014, the European Space Agency (ESA) made two big accomplishments for the first time in history. It put the Rosetta spacecraft into orbit around the **comet** 67P. The ESA then put a lander on the comet's surface.

There was soon a conspiracy theory that the mission's success was not as it seemed. A website reported an email from an "ESA insider." It revealed that the **probe** may not have landed on the comet at all.

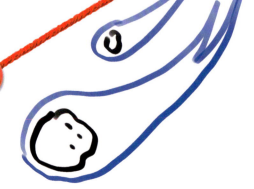

It took seven hours for the lander (middle) to leave the spacecraft and reach the comet's surface.

The source claimed that NASA had received mysterious radio signals from the direction of this comet. The email included photos that showed machinelike parts and possible structures on the comet's surface.

Some people decided this was not a comet, but an alien object. They thought the signals could have been a greeting to humans from aliens. Scientists then may have decided to investigate the source and send the spacecraft there.

Conspiracy theory supporters also say two photos from the Rosetta spacecraft show unidentified flying objects (UFOs) flying near the comet. The photos are also said to show a tower-like structure that could have been sending out the signals.

Experts say there is no reason to believe 67P is not a comet. There is no proof the comet is connected to aliens. The structures said to be in the photos are hard to see clearly. The mission was not planned to investigate signs of aliens. It was done to learn more about comets. The ESA did confirm that some sounds or signals were coming from comet 67P. Experts believe these were caused by movement of particles around the comet.

Photos from Rosetta's lander revealed the appearance of 67P's surface.

The Rosetta mission crew closely watched as the lander reached the comet.

Huge Challenges

The Rosetta mission was a challenge to plan and carry out. The spacecraft traveled 4 billion miles (6.4 billion km) on its journey. The comet was traveling 84,000 miles (135,000 km) per hour. The team had to launch and control the probe from Earth. The probe landing did not go as planned. Spear-like objects called harpoons were supposed to pin the probe to the surface. But they didn't launch. The probe then bounced off the surface. It came close to falling off an icy cliff!

Chapter 5

NEMESIS, ASTEROIDS, AND REMAINING QUESTIONS

Could an unseen star be putting **asteroids** or comets on a collision course with Earth? Some scientists say a much smaller and dimmer star is orbiting the sun. It's called Nemesis and is said to be the sun's "evil twin." However, this star has not been found. People think its orbit takes it a long distance from Earth. Some people have suggested that Nemesis's gravity may affect the paths of comets and asteroids. They think Nemesis could cause these to hit Earth.

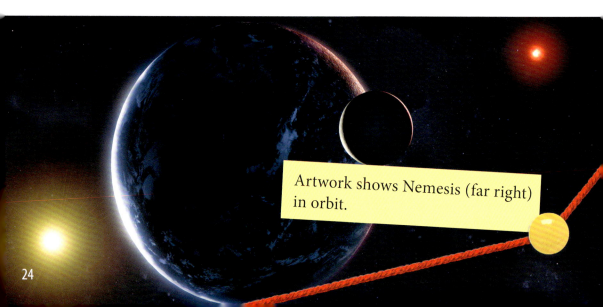

Artwork shows Nemesis (far right) in orbit.

People have used the Nemesis theory as a way to explain why asteroids have collided with Earth. NASA says there has never been any evidence that there is another star in our **solar system**.

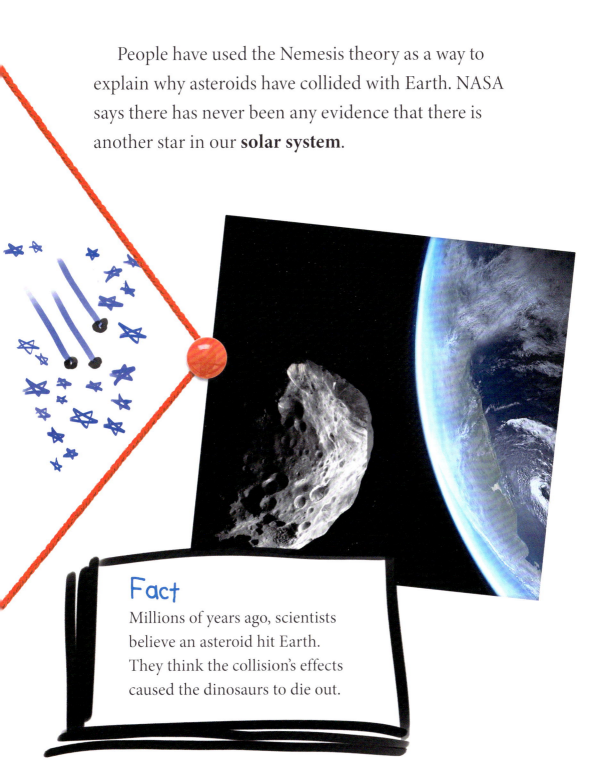

Fact

Millions of years ago, scientists believe an asteroid hit Earth. They think the collision's effects caused the dinosaurs to die out.

Conspiracy theories often warn of objects that will collide with Earth. They say governments or other groups know the objects are coming, but they don't tell the public. In 1976, a book claimed that the ancient Sumerians had written about a planet named Nibiru. Nibiru was said to orbit the sun every 3,600 years. Later, a **psychic** said that aliens had warned her that this planet would collide with Earth in 2003.

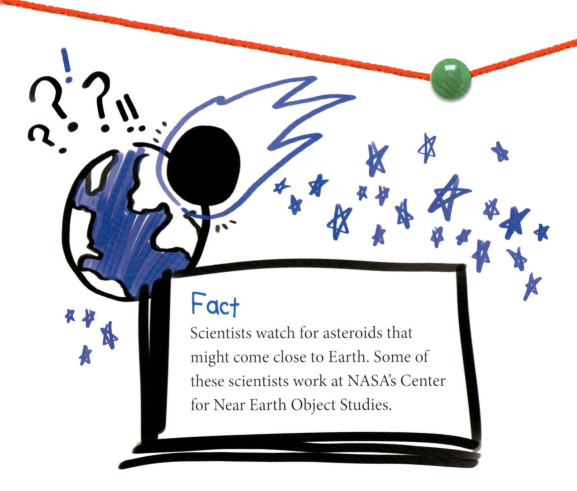

Fact
Scientists watch for asteroids that might come close to Earth. Some of these scientists work at NASA's Center for Near Earth Object Studies.

Artwork of Nibiru next to Earth

When this collision did not happen, the date was changed to 2012. Supporters of the conspiracy theory claimed that NASA was covering up this information. NASA responded that no large planet would destroy Earth in 2012. They were proven right. No **astronomers** reported seeing the mythical planet.

Astronomers who study stars and planets often admit that they don't know everything. Sometimes, scientists do not yet have enough proof to agree that a theory is correct. This can lead to conspiracy theories as some people claim scientists know more than they are saying to the public.

NASA is building equipment for its Artemis missions. These missions will send astronauts to the moon.

Many conspiracy theories can be easily disproven. Scientists have gathered a great deal of information about space. It can be used as evidence. However, some theories are more difficult to disprove. They place doubts in our minds.

Although conspiracy theories are often false, they can be useful. They remind us that it's important to ask questions. Scientists are always asking questions. Scientific knowledge continually changes.

The next time you hear about a conspiracy theory, do research. Ask questions and look for agreed-upon explanations that scientists provide. By investigating thoroughly, you can decide more easily whether a conspiracy theory can be disproven or not.

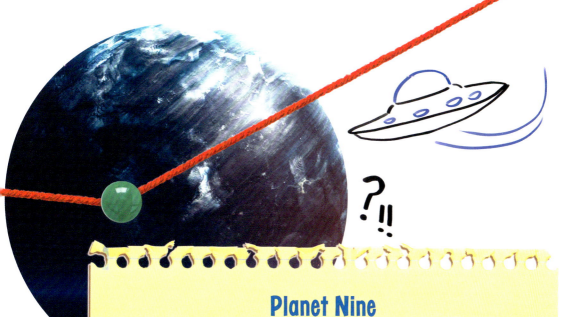

Planet Nine

The mysterious Planet Nine, or Planet X, is an example of a scientific theory that has not yet been proven. Many scientists believe that Planet Nine could be on the edge of our solar system. This planet would be very far from the sun. Very little light would reach it. So far, scientists have not been able to spot it. They have used only math models to suggest it exists. However, something on the solar system's edge is affecting the way some small planets and other objects cluster together in orbit.

Glossary

astronomer (uh-STRAH-nuh-muhr)—a scientist who studies stars, planets, and other objects in space

atmosphere (AT-muh-sfeer)—the layer of gases that surrounds some planets, dwarf planets, and moons

comet (KAH-muht)—an object of rock and ice that circles the sun

evidence (EV-uh-duhnss)—information, items, and facts that help prove something to be true or false

glitch (GLICH)—an unexpected small problem

gravity (GRAV-uh-tee)—a force that pulls objects with mass together; gravity pulls objects down toward the center of Earth

microbe (MYE-krobe)—a living thing that is too small to see without a microscope

orbit (OR-bit)—to travel around an object in space; an orbit is also the path an object follows while circling an object in space

parallel (PA-ruh-lel)—to be in a straight line and an equal distance apart

probe (PROHB)—a spacecraft sent to gather data

psychic (SYE-kik)—someone who claims to be able to tell what people are thinking or to predict the future

rover (ROH-vur)—a small vehicle that people can move by using remote control; rovers are used to explore objects in space

solar system (SOH-lurh SISS-tuhm)—a system of planets and other bodies orbiting the sun

Read More

Chandler, Matt. *The Apollo 11 Moon Landing: Spot the Myths*. North Mankato, MN: Capstone, 2024.

Gravel, Elise. *Killer Underwear Invasion!: How to Spot Fake News, Disinformation & Conspiracy Theories*. San Francisco: Chronicle, 2022.

Harman, Alice. *Life on Other Worlds*. New York: PowerKids Press, 2021.

Thompson, V. C. *The Moon Landing Was Fake*. Ann Arbor, MI: 45th Parallel Press, 2023.

Internet Sites

ESA Kids: The Rosetta Mission
esa.int/kids/en/Multimedia/Videos/Rosetta_animations/The_Rosetta_Mission

NASA: Hypothetical Planet X
solarsystem.nasa.gov/planets/hypothetical-planet-x/in-depth/

Royal Museums Greenwich: Moon Landing Conspiracy Theories, Debunked
rmg.co.uk/stories/topics/moon-landing-conspiracy-theories-debunked

Index

Aldrin, Buzz, 9, 11, 12
aliens, 14, 15, 18, 21, 22, 26
Armstrong, Neil, 8, 9, 12

comets, 20, 21, 22, 23, 24
Curiosity rover, 17

European Space Agency (ESA), 20, 22

face on Mars, 15, 16
flags, 10, 11, 12

gravity, 5, 24

International Space Station (ISS), 4, 5

Lunar Reconnaissance Orbiter (LRO), 12

microbes, 19

National Aeronautics and Space Administration (NASA), 6, 9, 12, 15, 16, 17, 18, 19, 21, 25, 26, 27, 28
Nemesis, 24, 25
Nibiru, 26, 27

Perseverance rover, 18
Planet Nine, 29

rocks, 12, 17
Rosetta spacecraft, 20, 21, 22, 23

shadows, 10, 16
solar system, 25, 29
sounds, 22
sun, 10, 16, 24, 26, 29

unidentified flying objects (UFOs), 22

videos, 5, 6
Viking 1 mission, 15, 19

About the Author

Nick Hunter has written more than 100 books for young people, including several on space and space exploration. He believes that humans did go to the moon and that scientists will find proof that there is life on Mars. Nick lives in Oxford, UK, with his wife and two sons.